Grace

Pocket Liturgies

Published 2007 by Proost
www.proost.co.uk

Copyright of liturgies
© Individual authors

Selection and arrangement of liturgies: Jonny Baker
Cover photo: Jonny Baker
Cover design: Jon Birch

ISBN 978-1-906340-00-1

To all who have been part of the Grace journey

Forward

The communities that are contributing to this series of
Pocket Liturgies have gifted the church with some of the
most amazing and wonderfully creative worship. We're
delighted to be able to publish them for a wider audience.
We hope they spark your own imagination and creativity.
These pieces are truly liturgy because they have emerged
out of the life of a community. They are 'the work of the
people' which is what the word liturgy means. Grace is an
alternative worship community in London that has inspired
people all round the world with its imaginative worship.
Words are one dimension of the worship. Were you to visit
Grace you would find images, video loops, music, rituals,
stations, installations and usually a café and conversation
to finish. So you'll have to imagine the other dimensions.
But the words carry weight. If you like what you find visit
the Grace web site www.freshworship.org where there is
an ever expanding archive of Grace liturgies.

Proost

Introduction

We have recently been through a process of re-evaluating Grace. We summed up several weeks of reflection, thought and prayer into three words:

Create, Participate and Engage

And as we learned more about Jesus and our community we found that there were new possibilities in an old situation. And where we might previously have made an easy, obvious choice, following the rules of our tradition, we became aware of new options in old situations. And we found that our new option had the word "truth" written all over it. But the word "truth" is hard to take. The truth might be uncomfortable. The truth might mean changes we hadn't anticipated which would shake us out of complacency. We added a fourth word:

Risk

We became aware that any given situation has a choice of doors to go through - the obvious, familiar one, and the new one you're vaguely aware of. That second door is smaller and harder to find than the familiar big door of comfort and self-satisfaction. The second door is not directly in front of us - it is in semi-darkness and may be covered in cobwebs until we turn around and find it. But as we reach out for the second door we find that the word "truth" is suddenly a lot more attractive. We find that the decision to reach for the other door has somehow given us a sense of being "bigger".

If we go through that door, and take the hard option, we find that we were wrong about the fear of the small, restricting room of the truth ... we find the biggest surprise that our hearts can contain ... because on the other side of the small, dimly lit door is a wide open space. And that wide open space is freedom ... it is the Realm of God.

Once we've been through that door we get used to its feeling, and in more and more situations we begin to see the second, smaller door, and we realise that the big door that we're used to going through actually led to a small room ... a kind of prison. Now that we're learning to find the small door, we are starting to know the price of putting our ethos centrally into the life of Grace. The first liturgy was written as part of a service launching a new season at Grace recommitting to our ethos. It builds on two previous doors liturgies and seems a fitting opener to Grace Pocket Liturgies [volume 1 we trust]. Some of our other liturgies are included in the book Alternative Worship.

Grace

Doors [3]

We will not allow our gifts and talents to be hidden
We will enter the Kingdom through the door marked "create"

We will encourage all to contribute
Our ideas are a gift offered to God
We will enter the Kingdom through the door marked "participate"

We will be hospitable and supportive to one another, to visitors and to the wider church. We will engage with everyday life and connect with culture.
We will enter the Kingdom through the door marked "engage"

We will not be afraid to fail but will push at our boundaries and try new things
We will enter the Kingdom through the door marked "risk"

We will go through these doors in the power of the Spirit knowing that Jesus has gone through them all first

Grace Ethos Confession

When our thoughtless criticism stifles the creativity of
others,
Lord, have mercy.
Lord, have mercy

When we keep a tight hold on power and deny others the
chance to participate.
Christ, have mercy.
Christ, have mercy.

When we prefer the safety of our holy huddle to the
wideness of God's world.
Christ, have mercy.
Christ, have mercy.

When we decline to take risks for fear that we might fail.
Lord, have mercy.
Lord, have mercy.

But when we praise the gifts of others,
share the power that we are given,
engage with communities beyond the boundaries of
our comfort,
and risk everything we have for the sake of others,
then, God rejoices in us.

Almighty God,

who forgives all who truly repent,

Have mercy upon *us*,

pardon and deliver *us* from all our sins,

confirm and strengthen *us* is all goodness,

and keep *us* in life eternal,

through Jesus Christ our Lord.

Amen.

Miracles

Lord God,

You spoke into darkness and chaos and then there
was light;

You imagined this earth in its complexity and beauty and
called it into being

You created humanity in your own image and gave us a
home to live in

We believe you can do miracles

But even if you don't, you are still God

Lord God,

You walked with Shadrach, Meshach and Abednego
through the fiery furnace

You shut the mouths of hungry lions and kept Daniel safe
until morning

You gave Hannah a family when she despaired of ever
having a child

We believe you can do miracles

But even if you don't, you are still God

Lord God,

You changed water into wine so the wedding party
could continue

You calmed a storm and your disciples with words of
quiet authority

You transformed a boy's picnic into a meal for a multitude
with plenty left over
We believe you can do miracles
But even if you don't, you are still God

Lord God,
You healed a woman from 12 years of bleeding
and rejection
You asked Bartimaeus what he wanted and then restored
his sight
You watched a paralysed man being lowered through
the roof and helped him to his feet
We believe you can do miracles
But even if you don't, you are still God

Lord God,
You called Lazarus from the tomb and restored him to life
You walked past the mourners at Jairus' house and gave
his daughter back to him
You suffered a horrendous crucifixion in order to defeat sin
and death and give us life
We believe you can do miracles
But even if you don't, you are still God

Lord God,
You told your disciples that they would do greater things
than you had done

We hear and read stories of miracles in our world - of you healing the sick, setting prisoners free, releasing drug addicts from their addiction, providing the right amount of money at just the right time

We believe you can do miracles

But even if you don't, you are still God

And yet, Lord, we don't see many miracles happening around us

We have friends with cancer, and we pray, and they are not healed

We have friends who long for children, and we pray, and they do not conceive

Our doubt is mixed with faith

Our trust is accompanied by questions

We acknowledge the mystery of faith and prayer, and the ways in which they are connected

We acknowledge that you often do things differently to the way we would do them

We long to know you better, to understand more of your ways

And we believe you can do miracles

But even if you don't, you are still God

Lord we believe.

Help our unbelief

The Invitation of God

We are creatures of comfort.
We like to be safe and secure
to be surrounded by what we know
to be in control
to order our lives in the way that suits us.

We want our journeys mapped out for us
itinerary decided, tickets booked
time of arrival guaranteed
refreshment breaks at regular intervals
and a credit card for unforeseen circumstances.

But Jesus said 'follow me' without saying where he
was going
just promising transformation along the way.

The Israelites in the desert, rescued from slavery and
oppression, were tired and homeless, hungry and thirsty,
insecure and unsettled.
And their minds went back to what they had known.
They yearned for the structure of predictable slavery
rather than the broken walls of unknown freedom.

Liminal space is the place of inbetweenness, of insecurity.
It is the Israelites in the wilderness,

It is Paul blind in Damascus waiting for Ananias.
Liminal space is emptiness and nowhere,
it is uncertainty and chaos,
it is a place of discomfort and unrest.
Liminality is a place of dying and rebirth, of
metamorphosis, the place where the caterpillar spins its
cocoon and disappears from view.

Nothing good or creative emerges from business as usual.
Much of the work of God is to get people into liminal space
and to keep them there long enough so they can learn
something essential.

This is the invitation of God, to move
-   from comfort to insecurity
-   from what we know to what we have yet to discover
-   from what we are good at to what we might fail at
-   from safety to a place of risk

Far I Have Come Far I Must Go

God of broken people and broken places
We confess to you our love of comfort,
of the known and predictable,
of the safe and secure.
We recognise that you call us into liminal space
To leave what we know and venture with you into desert
and wilderness, into blindness and discomfort
We want to follow you, but it's hard to leave what we know
Help us to trust you, and to set out.

On the journey of faith,
Far I have come, far I must go

God of broken people and broken places
We thank you for all that Grace has been to us and to
many others
We thank you for the space to listen, to grow, to create, to
be challenged
We recognise that you are calling us on
To leave what we know and venture with you into new
things, into engagement and participation, into creativity
and risk, into new structures and opportunities
We want to follow you, but it's hard to leave what we know
and we're not sure where we're going
Help us to trust you, and to set out.

On the journey of faith,

Far we have come, far we must go.

God of rebuilt people and rebuilt places

You have plans for deserts and wilderness

'Water will gush forth in the wilderness and streams

in the desert.

The burning sand will become a pool,

The thirsty ground bubbling springs.

In the haunts where jackals once lay,

Grass and reeds and papyrus will grow.

And a highway will be there; it will be called the Way of

Holiness.'

God of transformation we look forward to what you will do

With our lives and with Grace

On the journey of faith,

Far we have come, far we must go.

Dreams Take Flight

Summer Is Over
Summer is over,
an end to sitting on the fence
A voice beneath your certainties
shakes the settled patterns
like a colder breeze that heralds distant winter

Strange lands lie waiting
beyond your southern horizon
Summer is over,
and you must go or perish
here in a world no longer yours
or on the way, but in hope
your star and compass often dark
glimpsed briefly between clouds

At journey's end, another summer
not like the first one
new seeds, new fruit to refresh the migrant
burnt by life between summers
warmed for a season
until the north calls again

Like the inner call of the migrating bird, where does God
call you?

Where is your bird migrating to?

What do you want to do for God?

What do you need along the way?

Accompanying ritual:

Take one of the sheets of paper and write your hopes and prayers for the journey ahead on the reverse side. Then fold them to make origami birds and hang them from washing lines to pray for our dreams to fly.

Accompanying Prayer:

Sometimes we can have dreams and plans for our lives that we just outgrow.

Sometimes we can have dreams and goal that were founded on grand ideas. But like the seed on rocky soil, they sprout up quickly and then wither; it seems right for them to die.

And then there are those dreams, visions, aspirations, that are planted so deeply in us that they can feel like part of God's dreams for us. No matter how low the flame is burning, no matter how little the shoot has sprouted since the seed first took root in our being, our heart still sings out somewhere when we bring it back to mind.

These are the dreams that we want to take flight, to re-engage with the great migration.

Dear God
Just as you don't break a bruised reed or snuff out a smouldering wick, graciously let our plans and dreams take flight.

Give us a sense of how we can coax them back to life
Incubate them

Let us see a next step
and the manageable close at hand
and the glorious dream far off.

We pray in the name of Jesus Christ. Amen

Spirit Labyrinth

A labyrinth is a walking meditation with three stages - the journey in; the centre; and the journey out. Spirit Labyrinth is one for Pentecost. As it is a summer festival (in the UK) we made a grass labyrinth.

Mowing Instructions
1. Decide on a labyrinth design. We picked one that looked relatively simple and was based on a pattern of circles.

2. Get your kit together - a mower (we had one with blades of 40cm width which worked well), a tape measure, some small sticks or tent pegs for marking it out, some pieces of string, some longer sticks, a cricket stump or equivalent, and a piece of washing line.

3. On a diagram of the labyrinth work out your measurements. Bang the cricket stump in the centre point.

Tie the washing line round it and then tie pieces of string on the washing line to mark the distance from the centre of each circle. The centre can be as big as you like. But each circle after that needs to be the width of the mower blades plus enough width for the lines in between the path. We went for about 8 inches on top of the width of the blades, which seemed about right. Once you have done this, with the washing line taut move it round in a circle and put tent pegs/small sticks to mark all your circles out.

4. With your diagram in front of you work out where the turns are and place your longer sticks there so that when you are mowing you don't cross a line you shouldn't and so that you know where to turn.

5. Follow the path from the entrance and always mow against the outer edge of the circles. Go slowly and carefully especially at a turn. If in doubt stop and look at the diagram to check it is correct. It is easiest with two people – one to mow and one to give instructions.

6. Having mowed the whole path go over it once more.

7. That's it - a beautiful labyrinth

Guidelines for walking Spirit Labyrinth that we gave to people

† life is a journey - as you walk reflect on your life's journey and your relationship with God

† walk slowly

† avoid the temptation to chat with others on the journey

† use the journey in to the centre to quiet down, to slow down, to let go of busyness and stress, to confess sin and ask forgiveness, and to prepare to meet with God

† as you walk be aware of others on the journey - pray for them

† sometimes you will be close to the centre and sometimes close to the edge - are you close or far from God on your journey?

† as you reach the centre this is holy space - a space to be with God in prayer

† in the centre there is some oil - this is a sign of the Spirit

† the person in front of you will anoint you with oil and pray for you to be filled afresh with the Spirit of God - receive, stay there as long as you like

† listen - is there something God might be saying to you?

† if someone comes in to the centre while you are there anoint them with oil and pray for them to be filled afresh with the Spirit of God

† when you are ready begin the journey out - as you do, take your encounter with God with you back into the world

† pray for the presence of God in the situations you are facing in everyday life

† as you finish the journey offer yourself afresh to God

Communion By Numbers

Communion began in the context of a meal. This liturgy takes it back into that setting. It is designed to work around small tables of about 8 people set up in a café style. On each table are a series of numbered envelopes that you have prepared in advance. Every time a bell rings the table open the next numbered envelope and follow the instructions. The sequence of envelopes follows a basic liturgical structure of a communion service. Welcome people with an initial drink and explain how the service will run. Then have someone keep an eye on the flow of the service to ring the bell when people seem ready to move on. This service could be adapted in lots of ways. Be creative with it – it's the power of a good idea. These were the envelopes we used first time.

1. Introduce yourselves, slips of paper with questions to ask each other
2. Iconic candle making kit with a night light, strip of acetate with the last supper image on and two paper clips. Give thanks for things that have happened this week.
3. Text a confession on your mobile phone to a prearranged number prefacing it with the word confess. An absolution with the words "you are forgiven" is triggered by the keyword confess. This was set up using a service

provided by an internet company. You could equally use another confession activity.

4. Read story of Thomas - share stories of doubt and surprise

5. Peace - toast glasses proposing a toast of affirmation to someone round the table.

6. Share what you are thankful for about Jesus. Share what you want to remember about Jesus. Use the images of Christ enclosed to spark discussion

7. Share bread and wine round the table after listening to the Eucharistic prayer (see communion prayer below). A bottle of wine and bread were already in place on each table. (How you share bread and wine may depend on your church tradition. Grace is in an Anglican church so had an ordained minister pray the prayer below and break the bread.)

8. Invite the group to share concerns for prayer - take one of the night lights and light it for each prayer.

9. Go and collect a plate of hot towels (the kind you get after a curry - we got some from a warehouse locally!) - say a blessing and use the towel as a sign of receiving the blessing.

Communion Prayer (used for communion by numbers)

Word becomes flesh
flesh becomes bread
bread becomes body
body becomes word

God is bread
bread is broken
pain becomes wine
wine becomes joy

Wine bursts the wineskins
God bursts the tomb
bread bursts into song

Holy, holy, holy…

We Hang Our Lives On Your Mercy

We hang our lives upon your mercy
measured out in miles
your boundaries and pathways,
co-ordinates and charts
that guide our steps
along roads you travelled before us

We will make time for you and your word
We will practice your ways until they are part of us
We will rest and play in you
We will be your people

We are not complete without one another
We cannot run the race alone

We will support one another
encourage one another
wait for the weak
pick up the fallen
through your strength and love

When we are together we will remember what it is like to
travel alone

When we are alone we will remember what it is like to travel together
Wherever we are we will remember God who always goes with us

Go with us now, Lord, this night and always.   Amen

Psalms

A series of two services focused on Psalms. The first was an exploration of ten psalms. The second was our own psalms created by people in Grace. These are a couple of the offerings.

A-Z [An Acrostic Psalm]

All praise to you Lord!

Because of you all things are made.

Creation is the greatest gift of all -

Don't doubt it!

Everything is made by you - from the

Flowers and the animals to the

Grass on the fields.

Hallelujah!

In our wildest dreams we couldn't have come up with the

Joys you have made

King of Kings

Lord of Lords.

Many have tried but

No one is greater than you.

Others may be undecided whether to

Praise you or

Question you but I

Rejoice in your

Salvation and

Trust you

Unquestionably. You are

Very reliable and we

Worship you for your

e**X**ceptional work.

You are the first and the last – the A-

Z

Psalm 23 Remixed

[David was a shepherd. These weren't just words on a page to David, but experiences that would have held a deep resonance for him. Which of the roles that I have in life does God fulfil for me, but much better?]

The Lord is my mother; I shall not be in want.

She makes me lie down in fresh clean sheets and tucks me in and kisses me goodnight, and while I sleep she sorts everything out, ready for the morning.
She makes me cups of tea and ginger cake when I get home from school, and shepherds pie for supper with plenty of fresh vegetables.

She leads me away from the TV to the kitchen table where we have space to talk without interruptions.
She listens to even the smallest of my worries and helps me get things in perspective.
She restores my soul.

She guides me through the mysteries of how to be a righteous woman,
for her name's sake.

Even though I walk past the bus stop
where the big boys threaten me

and the bitchy girls laugh at me,
I will fear no evil for you are with me.
Your strength beside me and your hand in mine,
they comfort and sustain me.

You prepare Sunday lunch for me in the presence
of my enemies,
to remind me that I'll always have a place to belong.

You have every confidence in me and my future;
you are my champion and my biggest fan.

My life overflows with the love you have given me
from my very first breath to my first grey hair and beyond.

Surely goodness and mercy shall follow me all the
days of my life
and I shall dwell in the house of the Lord forever.

Slow

Slow was a liturgy inspired by Kosoke Koyama's book
Three Mile an Hour God in which he suggests that God's
pace is walking pace. This is quite a contrast to the pace
of life in London and we were drawn to the idea of
exploring this in Grace.

The layout for the liturgy was that the room had two
screens back to back in the centre of the room. On one
side were projected images of slow and the other side
images of speed.

Slow Intro

[Invite people to take watches off/turn phones off]

The service is entitled slow, but you can't talk about slow without considering its opposite. It's not as simple as saying slow is good and fast is bad - slow is bad when you're waiting for an ambulance, but good when you're waiting for the dentist.

[Explain fast and slow ends of room]

Take a few moments to consider your feelings about fast and slow

Are you a fast person or a slow person?
Do you want to slow down or speed up?
Is your life already fast or slow?
Are you in a fast place or a slow place - spiritually, mentally, physically?
Do you want to be in a faster place or a slower place?
How fast or slow do you want to get there?

Do you seek slow love and fast food? or vice versa?
Is work too fast and travel too slow? or vice versa?
Are you a contemplative trapped inside a commuter?
If the motorway is empty do you slow down or speed up?
Is your computer too slow or too fast?

Slow opening liturgy

To those who creep towards the kingdom

God says welcome

To those who rush towards the kingdom

God says welcome

To all of you, however you come, in speed and sloth,

God says welcome

To the door and the arms that are always open wide

[Play Tourist with the line 'Hey Man Slow Down' by Radiohead]

Slow-ometer – Flat Out to Flat Out

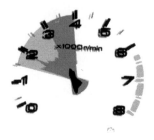

At what speed do you live your life?

Always in a rush or slowly getting bored?

And at what speed would you like to live your life?

Where would you place yourself on the slow-ometer?

0.03mph	Garden snail
0.15mph	Three toed sloth
0.17mph	Giant tortoise
11mph	Pig
25mph	Elephant
30mph	Urban speed limit
40mph	Mongolian wild ass
70mph	Cheetah
200mph	Peregrine Falcon
1340mph	Concorde
334 million mph	Lightning
700 million mph	Speed of light in vacuum
8.3 billion mph	Santa's sleigh

Slow Meditation

Reality is a static image, rolling past at 24 frames
per second
If we slow the movie down, what will we see?

Slow the projector in your head and lose the fluidity
Embrace the flicker, the jerkiness
Allow the frames of your life to disconnect and stop

Now your life lies still in front of your eyes, what do
you see?
Play 'spot the difference' with each frozen moment
Now you have time to examine carefully each corner and
shadow what details are revealed, that you always move
too fast to see?

Fleeting expressions and imperceptible gestures
betraying a truth not discerned
a turning you didn't take
another universe of futures, vanishing from sight

To us the stars stand still
but ancient eyes could not navigate by our skies
The north point of the sky moves in a circle
28000 years around

The north star we know is not the north star of our
ancestors or descendants
They will see other constellations

Does God see our lives the way we see the stars?
Innumerable slow movements plotted and understood on
charts long before the event
constellations drawn that serve for a while and break up
How slow is reality for God?
What do fast and slow mean in eternity
where every tiny moment and endless age are available
for detailed inspection
A day like a thousand years,
and a thousand years like a day

If we slow down do we see more like God sees?
See all the details
creation's crazy minutiae
Who would have time to see all that stuff except God?
Is that why there's so much of it?

How quickly does salvation come?
If we slowed our lives down would we see every step
and progression?
Or would its detail still evade us
a blur of motion in the shadows of a static frame
a frozen block in the centre of the movie?

If we slow down will we see what God sees?

Will we see what God is doing?

Have you ever tried?

Slow Confession

O God, you are slow to anger and swift to have mercy;
Forgive us when we treat time as a commodity
or an enemy,
when we abuse your gift of time.

In our fastness and our slowness,
help us to keep pace with you.
Free us to live in your time, a new time,
in which there is a time for everything under heaven,
and slow is not too slow, and fast is not too fast.

Transform us into people who see time as a gift
and a friend,
who live as if we have time,
because we know that your time will never cease.
Through Jesus we pray, Amen.

Slow Blessing

God the creator, who rested on the seventh day after the work was done, show you how to balance the slow and the fast, the work and the rest.

God the redeemer, who lived his life at walking pace, strengthen you to go slow when the world is going fast.

God the sustainer, who came at Pentecost like a rushing wind, give you hope in the day when there will be freedom from the limitations of time.

Go into a world of speed and live at God's pace.

Amen.

Concluding Ritual

Invite people to take a hard boiled sweet to suck if they want to respond by slowing down, or to take a soft chewy sweet if they want to respond by speeding up.

Ad Liturgy

[This liturgy was part of a series exploring how to live as Christians in a consumer culture. All the response lines are slogans from ads. It is inevitably dated by the moment in which it is written.]

We live after purity
True

In a world of rich and poor, global warming, information overload, cafe direct, nike and gap
You either love it or you hate it

Our life is complex and interlinked not simple and straightforward
It's as clear as your conscience

Our actions and choices have a knock on effect for others - neighbours near home and far away
Help us in this context to follow you
Always

When our thoughts are filled with dreams of wealth and objects of desire
Think different

When we reach information overload
Have a break

Take some space and time
Everyone needs a place to think

Help us use our withdrawal as a time to learn to love the world more
Stop liking start loving

Make us angry about injustice and determined to make a difference
Just do it

Help us know which concerns to make our own
Because life is complicated enough

When apathy sets in to remember
Every little helps

When individual actions seem too small to count, thank you that we are part of your body, the largest global network
Together we are stronger

Give us patience when change is slow
Good things come to those who wait

We long to see your kingdom come
The future's bright

And your will be done
Whatever it takes

On earth as it is in heaven
A taste of paradise

To the glory of God
Because he's worth it!

New Year Examen

The Examen is a prayer practice, articulated and made popular by a man who came to be known as Ignatius of Loyola – born in the late 15th C in Northern Spain. It is, in short, a way of listening to ourselves and to God. It is a practice of listening contemplatively to our own lives. It is a tool for discerning the presence and absence of God in our lives.

St Ignatius in his teaching of the Examen expected that God would speak through our deepest feelings and yearning, what he called consolation and desolation. Consolation is whatever helps us to connect in love to ourselves, others, God and the universe. In his language – whatever leads to an increase in faith, hope and love. Desolation is whatever blocks that connection…

So what follows is this – if we can reflect upon what in our life connects us to Life, love, faith, hope, peace… the qualities of the spirit… we can track where it is God is most available to us – or, more precisely, where we are most available to God. And the opposite – if we can see where it is we are being drained of life – and then think about how we block God in those areas… This is not the same as feeling merely good or bad.

The Examen is traditionally done on a daily basis – but can usefully be applied to all sorts of other times – This is an Examen of the last year as a way of entering this New year with more awareness of where God is speaking to you in your life…and where you find yourself being drawn away from God's love.

Examen of the Year

Begin to let yourself remember the last year…
don't try too hard…
At first, just scan the year and get a sense of it.…
Christmas and the time leading up to it.… Autumn……
Summer…… Spring….. the year…..

Now let come what comes at first when you ask the questions:

When did I feel best able to give and receive love?
What caused in me an increase in faith, hope and love?
Where was I drawn to God?
In fears, in joy, in pain, in creativity?
In prayer, in liturgy, scripture, creation?
In work or leisure?
In family, friend, colleague, church community, neighbour?

Did I feel myself being nudged or prompted in any particular way?

Out of all the year's experiences, is there one experience that I feel most grateful for?

Relish these moments of consolation – of revelation…. Give thanks.

Look again back over the year. When was I aware of God's absence? When did I feel least able to give or receive love?
What caused in me a decrease in faith, hope and love?
When did I fail to respond to His love at work in me?

Without harsh judgement, just let yourself look at that experience.

In the light of God's love – what would you like to say to God about that time, event, experience? What does God want to say to you?

And now, coming back into the present:

What insight, revelation, grace do I receive from the experiences of the last year?

Having reviewed the last year – what gift do I hold for the new year?
What would I like to bring into the New Year?

Find a word or a phrase or an image to represent what you'd like to bring into the New Year…

Keep that word or phrase or image in your heart over the next year. You might like to adapt this examen for use everyday or weekly.

Let's pray for the grace to move into this new year with love, faith and hope…. for the grace to bring more of what gives us life…. for the grace to continue to recognise God in our daily life….

Not In My Name Communion

Opening Prayer

We meet in the name of the God of mercy and
compassion

The God of justice and love

We meet in the name of the One who called himself the
bread and water of life

**The One who is always hungry for justice for all the
earth's people**

Procession of bread and wine

(brought to the table by a protest march)

We bring this gift of bread to the table of Christ

Bread, Christ's body, broken for our brokenness.

**As we share in one bread we draw closer to Christ and
to each other.**

We bring this gift of wine to the table of Christ

**Wine, Christ's blood, poured out for the healing of the
nations. As we share in Christ's death we are
reminded of who we are... One in Him, bringing hope
to the poor, and justice to the oppressed.**

No more stolen bread! No more spilt blood!

Not in my name

Will we fight terror with terror

Not in my name

Will we exploit the resources of those who are poorer

Not in my name

Will the bodies of the innocent be broken for the evils
of a few

Not in my name

Will we deny life to those for whom life is a struggle

Not in my name

Will the name of god be used as an excuse for our own
self interest

Not in my name

Will we be blinkered by our flawed sense of justice

Not in my name

Will the bread of life be robbed from the mouths of the
world's hungriest

Not in my name

Will we find salvation in the defeat of our enemies

Not in my name

Will our government wipe out innocent families

Not in my name

Will we reap reward from terrorism and invasion

Not in my name

Will the west get rich through the debts of the poor

**We thank Christ for his body broken and blood shed.
We acknowledge his sacrifice for the salvation and
redemption of the world.**

We acknowledge innocent blood shed and bodies broken to be enemies of God's kingdom and a sin against creation.
We acknowlege love, truth, grace, justice, righteousness, mercy and humility to be signatures of God's rule.
May God bless us as we seek to send a clear message to those in authority...
Not in my name!

Confession and Absolution
Listen to the words of the prophet Hosea:
The trader calls out to the Lord his God,
but in his hands are dishonest scales,
and in all he does he loves to oppress.
He calls out, 'Aha! I have become very rich
and no one can prove that I gained it by sin.'
And this is what the Lord replies:
'I see all that you have done.
Return to me, the Lord your God,
hold fast to love and justice,
and wait continually for your God.'
[Based on Hosea 12:6-8]

We are people who are eager to do well,
but slow to do good.
Let us return to the Lord our God;

In your mercy, Lord, forgive us.

We are people who are eager to save time, but slow to give time.
Let us return to the Lord our God;
In your mercy, Lord, forgive us.

We are people who are eager to improve our lives, but slow to improve our world.
Let us return to the Lord our God;
In your mercy, Lord, forgive us.

And still the world trades with dishonest scales.
Let us return to the Lord our God;
In your mercy, Lord, forgive us.

Hold fast to love and justice.
God forgives you,
Forgive yourselves,
Forgive others.

The Word
A selection of passages on justice

Communion Prayer
We come to remember the life and death of Jesus Christ
And we will not forget the life of all your children

We receive the promise of liberation in Jesus Christ

And we will promote freedom and justice for all God's people

We recall his life of protest, praise and love

And offer you our lives for uniting, not dividing, your world

May we not betray you

May we not betray them

Nor forget you

Nor forget them

Nor ignore you

Nor ignore them

At this holy feast where earth meets heaven

This holy place where there is room for all

We come with empty hands and open hearts

To share with people unseen from across your world

With people unseen from past and future

We meet at your crossroad of time and space

Revive us with life

Infuse us with love

At this holy feast

Where earth meets heaven

The table of Jesus

Where there is room for all

He whom the universe could not contain
Is present to us in this bread
[the bread is broken]

He who redeemed us and called us by name
Now meets us in this cup
[the wine is poured]

So take this bread and this wine
In them God comes to us
So that we may come to God

Sharing of bread and wine

Prayer after communion
Almighty God,
we thank you for feeding us
with the body and blood of your Son
Jesus Christ.
Through him we offer you our souls and bodies
our time and energy
our protest and praise
our willingness to lose our own lives
if that will bring your kingdom of mercy on earth
Send us out infected with your Holy Spirit of love
Inspired to change history for your praise and glory
Amen

Nine

Nine readings... nine tunes... nine surprises...

"Nine" is the Grace version of the traditional Advent service of nine lessons and carols. The nine lessons are there, but they are allocated randomly to nine volunteers, each with the task of producing their own reflection on the reading, which must include a piece of music. And so the story is told, from the first light of creation to the coming of the new light in Jesus.

In keeping with Advent, expect the unexpected. The music used has ranged from medieval carols to rock music. Contributions have included meditations on pictures, audiovisual pieces, participatory exercises, poems, and (once) an exercise inspired by "I'm a celebrity..."

1. Genesis 1, vv 1-5, 26-8, 31: The Creation
2. Genesis 3, vv 8-15, 17-19: The Fall
3. Isaiah 9, vv 2, 6, 7: The people who walked in darkness...
4. Isaiah 11, vv 1-3a, 4a, 6-9: Isaiah's vision of the kingdom
5. Luke 1, vv 26-35, 38: The Annunciation

6. Luke 2, vv 1, 3-7: The Nativity

7. Luke 2, vv 8-16: The Shepherds

8. Matthew 2, vv 1-12: The Magi

9. John 1, vv 1-14: The Word

Now the story has been told. Now is the time to go and live it! In the name of Christ, Amen.

Advent Waiting: How long would you wait?

Mark out a timeline on the floor with tape. Divide into 23 equal intervals which read:

1 second

2 seconds

30 seconds

1 minute

5 minutes

15 minutes

30 minutes

1 hour

3 hours

6 hours

12 hours

1 day

2 days

1 week

2 weeks

1 month

6 months

1 year

5 years

10 years

20 years

50 years

a lifetime

Make a set of cards each of which reads 'How long would you wait' and one of the following:

for a good idea?

for the government to reform the National Health Service?

for the punchline in a joke?

for someone to answer the phone?

for a shop assistant to serve you?

for a promise to be kept?

for a new car in your preferred colour?

for an answer to prayer?

for a red light to change before jumping it?

for a Big Mac?

for the bar staff to serve you?

for an ambulance?

in the checkout queue at a supermarket?

for a main course in a restaurant?

for a bus?

for the right partner to marry?

for a colleague at work to return your call?

for the lift in a department store?

for sex with someone you fancy?

for a web page to download?

for an apology before forgiving?

for delivery of a new sofa?

for a sign that someone loves you?

to meet the Queen?

for a plumber to fix your sink?

for a person in a coma before switching off the life
support machine?

for a prophecy to be fulfilled?

for your child to be obedient?

for a pay rise before changing jobs?

for a missing person to return before believing that
they're dead?

for engagement to lead to marriage?

to conceive before giving up?

to see your family doctor?

to meet the Prime Minister?

to meet Madonna?

for entry into a nightclub?

to meet Banksy?

for your favourite band to come onstage?

for a holiday flight without complaining?

for a date to show up?

for your lover to return before accepting that it's over?

for non-violence to work?

Place the cards along the timeline to give your answers.
The next person then gathers them up to do the same.

Gold Frankincense and Myrrh Confession

Holy God accept our prayers tonight
You asked for all of our being, our thoughts and actions,
our creativity and expression
What do we give you?
We think back two millenia to when the Christ child
was born
What would we give the baby?
What does a baby need?
What does the baby ask of us?
What gifts did the baby receive?

Gold - a gift for a king
A metal so precious that we have died and killed for it
We treat your creation like it wasn't our home
We've robbed the earth of its riches and left its wounds
open to infection
Forgive us for not giving you the best of us
What's the point of offering you the religious bits if the rest
is kept closely guarded?

Think of the best parts of your life
Give them to God

Frankincense - a gift for God
The fragrance of worship, God's eau de cologne

Worship giving God the honour that is due to him
Forgive our efforts to worship you only when it is
convenient to do so
And with people that we choose, making outcasts of our
brothers and sisters
Forgive us when our actions make our words of
worship meaningless

Think of your worship
Give it to God

Myrrh - a gift for a mortal
The smell of a cover up to hide death and decay
But nothing is hidden from you
Forgive us for denying the reality of pain, suffering and
struggle
Do we get angry and shout at God?
Or do we bury our pain?

Grace In The Making

Creativity and imagination are divine gifts that
get to the heart of what it is to be human,
God's image bearers.

It is of course possible to deny the gift
or grow out of the habit
or recite the mantras 'i'm not creative', 'i haven't got the
gift' or 'i haven't got time'
But such denial won't wash -
it's the road to numbness

Cook a meal
Plan a pilgrimage
Make some music
Form a garden
Pull off a skateboard trick
Tell a story
Take a picture
Design a web page
Write a prayer

Grace is in the making.

We have got used to passivity

to consuming what others have made

to sitting and watching

to processed and pre-packed

to fast food

to reality tv

Consuming isn't bad

It's what you do with it and who can get in the shops that's
the problem

Even shopping can be creative

Create

Make something

Surprise yourself

Play

Wake up

Encounter grace

Grace To be Seen

Grace comes to us through the senses

We touch it, or it touches us, in an embrace
We smell it in freshly baked bread and morning coffee
We hear it in the ocean or Massive Attack
We taste it in a strawberry or a cold belgian beer
We see it in the eyes of a child or the lines of an old
person's face

All our senses together like a huge neon sign saying
'LIFE IS A GIFT!'

This is how grace comes to us...
In the ordinary stuff of life, the everyday
Yet in our numbness it's easy to miss this most
simple of gifts
and go round with our eyes closed

Mystics speak of awareness and its connection
with prayer
Become aware of your own breath
Breathe in and feel the cold air on the hairs of your nostrils
Feel your pulse
Look at the skin on your hand

Slow down

Look around you

Notice details that you normally miss

amazing things in your everyday world that you often

walk by

Maybe God is in the detail we normally miss

You don't need eyes to see - you need vision

Windows: Icons of the Present

[For this service people were invited to bring an icon of the present to the worship service – something that functioned as an icon for them, whether a piece of art, a music track, a traditional icon or whatever.]

Intro

The characteristic of windows is that they let light through. The characteristic of icons is that they let the light of heaven through. Not that they have their own inner light, in an idolatrous or pagan fashion, but that under certain conditions [which we may not be able to summon or control] the light of the presence of God, of ultimate reality, shines through.

It's like an office block clad in tinted glass; during daytime the surface is opaque, it reflects back and we cannot see in; but at dusk as the lights come on inside the building, it becomes transparent; the solid-seeming glass melts away to reveal what was behind it all along.

Transfiguration would be another way of putting it; on the Mount of Transfiguration Jesus' humanity became transparent and the light of reality, of heaven, shone through it onto the disciples.

What is your window?

Invite people to bring their icons to the front to add to the altar. Ask them to explain if they would like to: how did it come to be an icon/window, when did they 'discover' it, how do they 'use' it?

Confession - the dirty window

We may not be able to summon or control this phenomenon; the light of heaven is often only visible in retrospect. At the time one was too preoccupied with earthly matters to see the presence of God, but afterwards looking back the situation seems bathed in God's light, and you wonder how you could not have seen it. The disciples probably felt the same way after the resurrection.

We often look through a glass darkly. We may not always be to blame for this, because the light is not ours to give. And certainly it's true that one person's window is another's sheet of ply, but often the light is shining, and we have blocked it out. We walk around with the curtains drawn, to prevent God seeing what goes on inside. Have you ever opened the curtains on a sunny morning, and noticed how dusty everything is? And yet you could pretend that the room was clean as long as the curtains were closed. The light brings the pain of housekeeping.

Perhaps the curtains are open, but the glass is dirty. Since we look through windows and not at them, it's easy not to notice until the window cleaner's been, and then we are surprised by how much brighter the colours of the garden are. Or perhaps you are looking through the net curtains of suspicion at what the neighbours are up to.

[Voice 1]
Lord of light, darkness is daylight to you.
Look into the windows of our souls
Draw back the curtains of indifference or shame, and let your light shine in;
take down the net curtains we use to keep up appearances, and make our lives unafraid and honest;
wipe off the smear and speck of sin, and let us see clearly into your kingdom.
Through Christ our Lord
Amen

Eucharist as icon
Your window may be round, square or arched but all look onto the same scene....

[Voice 2]
On the Lord's day I was in the Spirit, and there before me was a window standing open into heaven. And a voice like

a trumpet said "Come up here, and I will show you what must take place after this."

[Voice 3]
Eternal God
fling open the windows of our hearts
to the weather of your Spirit
lead us out beneath the dancing sky and wind
across the stumbling ground of our reality
to where the sound of worship never ceases
and the view stretches further than the human eye can see
through Christ the faithful witness
Amen

The eucharist is an icon
The eucharist is a window
In the eucharist the bread and the wine become
transparent to the presence of the risen Christ
This is a foretaste of the new heaven and the new earth
when all things will be transparent with his presence in the
same way, and all things will be sacraments to one
another, including we ourselves.

Eucharistic prayer
The Lord is here
God's Spirit is with us.....

After-communion prayer

Looking out through the window

[Voice 4]
Now that we have eaten bread that fed our inner vision
Now that we have sipped the wine that washed the
windows of our soul
the view from here is clearer
We see beauty and wrongdoing in true colours
No longer blurred together by the sin that clouded
conscience, like John we see the struggle, and know we
must take sides.

Father of all creation
Give your servants in all situations your wisdom and
strength, to choose the right path and to walk it.
Give us your protection as we walk your line
and may the vision of your presence be always in our
windows like a cloud of smoke by day and a pillar of
fire
by night.
Through Christ the icon of God
and the Spirit who gives sight
Amen

Bring Your Own Station

Part of the grace ethos is participation. Bring Your Own Station puts this to the ultimate test. The liturgy is the collection of stations brought by members of the community and set up before the service begins for people to experience and interact with. This works well with a strong seasonal theme so that people have plenty of ideas to work with. We first ran it for lent. Below is the text that we sent round which explains how it worked in practice. The two pieces that follow were stations – Entrance and Exit and Everyday Stones.

Text sent round describing Bring Your Own Station
Please bring a station with you on the theme of lent and/or a tune on an ipod or CD.

What is a station?
One of the sorts of service we do at grace involves walking around the worship space interacting with stations that have been set up in advance that contain something to cause you to reflect, pray, worship, think, or actively participate in a ritual. These might be as simple as lighting a candle, reading a story, writing a prayer, adding a stone to a pile, looking at a video loop, listening to a meditation,

tasting some fruit or whatever. If you've never done this before even better – this could be the start of something...

What do I do?

The theme is lent. Lent is a season of preparation for Easter typically focused on discipleship and following Christ. Do anything that relates to that. If you want to work from a scripture passage then three ideas to spin off from might be a) Jesus' temptations in the wilderness b) the return of the prodigal son c) Psalms. Create something that is self-contained for people to visit – i.e. it has things that people can engage with without you having to be there to explain it. So if there are instructions print them out for people to read and then add what you like in the way of things to look at or read, activities, small rituals, food for thought etc.

When will it be set up?

Please arrive early to set your station up. We will allocate you a space to set up. The earlier you are the more choice you will get.

What about the music?

We will have a CD player and ipod mixer. So if you have a tune (that relates to the lent theme in some way) bring it along and you can play it.

How will it actually work?

Grace will start at 8pm. Music that people bring will provide a soundscape while everyone walks round and interacts with the stations for as long as they like. Then when you're done the café wil be open as normal. It's that simple.

I'm not sure I can do anything up to standard

Please don't be shy or think what you do won't be good enough. It can be really simple. Just work with an idea. We value creativity, participation and risk so go for it.

I need help

If you want to bounce your idea off someone else or if you need some technical stuff (a TV or slide projector for example) then e-mail us

Do I need to let you know what I am doing in advance?

No. We quite like the element of surprise so do just turn up and set up your station.

Can I come if I haven't got a station?

Of course everyone is welcome whether or not you have done a station. But if we all think that way it may be a very short Grace!

Entrance and Exit

The Station consisted of a gate with a welcome mat and a screen with a collection of pictures of doors and gates. The accompanying text was printed on sheets of paper and people were invited to write their responses to the concluding question on a piece of paper and stick it to the gate.

Wherever you look there are entrances and exits - doorways in and doorways out. Each one marks out a different territory where particular rules apply. Each space on the other side of these thresholds, these boundaries, is the domain of someone.

I remember an aunt in the north of England who had a particular pride in keeping the doorstep polished and the kettle on. Her domain was a place of welcoming and hospitality but of course not all spaces are as welcoming as my aunt's. Some places are selectively welcoming, keeping out undesirable elements while only opening the doors to those who fit certain criteria.

The Celts used the idea of the open gate. I like to think that this image – a gate through which the land is visible, enticing and accessible – is a good way of understanding the gateway which is open to all who choose to venture that way. This is an idea which offers us all hope, but in order to go to one place we necessarily have to leave another – so the gateway is both an entrance and an exit.

So what do you want to leave behind and where do you want to go?

Everyday Stones

This was a simple station with stones next to a growing pile of stones and this text accompanying:

Jesus was hungry, really hungry.

Wanting bread, needing food, not unreasonable in the situation.

But Jesus wasn't tempted by bread to break his fast. Jesus was tempted by stones and the power he had to turn them into bread.

We all have legitimate needs and feelings of 'want' to express. Everyday we are faced with the same temptation as Jesus. To fulfil our needs and wants by small, easy actions that are within our power but we know are wrong.

What are your 'everyday stones'?

Leave the temptation behind,
as one of the pebbles on this pile.

Missional Turn

For this liturgy you need a table in the centre. Place some bread, a cross, and a candle on the table. You also need enough night light candles so that each person can have one each and some matches. This ritual came at the end of a service exploring how we become more missional in our community life. Invite people to gather in a circle around the table.

We have been exploring the ethos of grace over the last few weeks -
creativity - we love being creative
participation - grace is not something to consume but to get involved in
and engagement - the spirit gives us an outward impulse to engage in mission life, the world, culture and in our local communities.

If you are involved in Grace we hope you will find yourself being creative, involved and engaged - these things will rub off on us all. Or else they are just empty words.

We stand on the threshold of the future. God is beckoning us into the future.

Bread is the body of Christ - I invite you to eat bread as a symbol of your participation in the life of God and God's kingdom. (pass round the bread inviting people to take some to eat)

The cross is the symbol of Christ's passion - his self-giving love. To follow in the way of Christ is to live a passion-ate life. Christ is re-inviting us to be passion-ate, to follow in the way of self-giving love. I'm going to pass the cross around - hold it and in your heart recommit to the way of the cross, the way of passion, the way of self-giving love. (pass round the cross)

The candle is the light of the world - Christ has ignited a spark or a fire in us. I invite you to take a candle and light it as a sign that you recommit to being a godbearer, to carry God's light into the world.

We have this nice inward facing circle. This is part of our problem. We seem close to God when we are facing inwards. We have fallen for the trap of thinking God is in here. But God is out there. A reversal needs to take place. When we talked about our ethos, one word kept coming up that never made it in to the three but perhaps undergirds them all - risk. Following God is a risk. So finally I'm going to ask you a simple question from the baptism service 'do you turn to Christ?'. Respond 'I do' if you'd like to. And as you do turn and face outwards. Then stay for a minute or two in silence facing outwards asking God to lead you and us into the future

Do you turn to Christ? **I do**

Drinks Eucharist

[This communion prayer was written and used round the table in someone's home during a meal. At the part describing the cup people were invited to chink their glasses/bottles together]

It takes many different drinks to make one party
different in strength and purity
different in colour and taste
coming from different places
to be poured out together in celebration

Let Christ be the unity that binds them
in their finished state
as he is the root of the fruit that made them.

On the night of his arrest
Jesus and his friends held a party
in memory and celebration of how God set his people free
from all that had enslaved and oppressed them.

While they ate, Jesus took some bread, thanked God,
broke it and gave it to his friends saying
"Eat this, it is my body broken for you. Do this to
remember me."

Later when the party was ending he filled his glass,

thanked God and held it out to them saying,

"chink this all of you, this is my blood

spilt for you and many others

to mend the broken bond between God and humanity"

In this God-touched bread and wine

creation sees its bondage broken

sign of hope and foretaste of its freedom

Stations Of The Resurrection

This liturgy was inspired by Andrew Walker's book *Journey Into Joy*. He suggests that often it seems like the season of Easter is over by Easter Tuesday when in fact it goes on for several weeks. The book offers a suggestion for a way of focusing on the resurrection narratives as a series of stations.

station i - the discovery of the empty tomb john 20:1-10
station ii - the angel speaks to the women luke 24:4-8
station iii - christ appears to the virgin mary
station iv - christ appears to mary magdalene
john 20:11-18
station v - the denial of the resurrection matthew 28:11-15
station vi - the road to emmaus luke 24:13-35
station vii - christ appears to the disciples john 20:19-21a
station viii - christ appears to thomas john 20:24-29
station ix - the appearance on the shore of galilee
john 21:1-14
station x - the questions to peter john 21:15-19
station xi - the appearance on the mountain
matthew 28:16-20
station xii - the revelation to st paul acts 9:3-9
station xiii - the ascension acts 1:6-11
station xiv - pentecost acts 2:1-11

There's no scripture given for station iii - instead Andrew Walker has a quote from Ignatius of Loyola - here is how after Christ had risen body and soul from the sepulchre, he appeared to his blessed mother. She had brought him to birth, raised him, and had stood by him throughout the passion. Now he wants to share with her the joy of his resurrection.

The liturgy for this service is simply that we invite 14 people to create a station based on that resurrection narrative. A station might be simply a piece of art to look at or some readings, or an interactive ritual based on the story. For the liturgy people are invited to walk around the space and interact with the 14 stations in their own time and at their own pace.

We have done the same thing as well based on the more familiar Stations of The Cross.

Emmaus Liturgy

This service follows the narrative of the Emmaus Road story in Luke 24. At the beginning of the service the story is read and then people are invited to explore seven stations that follow the narrative as follows

Station 1: The hiddenness of God [Luke 24: 13-16]
This station is about the "dark night of the soul," and how the experience of the absence of God can be legitimate and not the result of sin. There are "magic eye/stereogram" books conveying the idea that God may be present, but we do not see. There is also the story from The Last Battle by C.S.Lewis of the dwarves who cannot see Aslan's kingdom.

Station 2: Downcast [Luke 24: 17-18]
This station contains the "bitter herbs" from the Passover meal. Worshipers are invited to taste these and read Psalm 22.

Station 3: Storytelling [Luke 24: 19-27] part 1
The disciples on the road to Emmaus were consoling one another by telling stories and remembering Christ. Worshippers are invited to write about a time in their life when they met with God, leaving their stories to be read by those who follow

Station 4: Storytelling [Luke 24: 19-27] part 2
About the power of hearing God's story, how this strengthens us in dark times. A CD player with headphones plays the track "Jesus' Blood Never Failed Me" by Gavin Briers.

Station 5: Welcoming the stranger [Luke 24: 28-29]
Who is the stranger for you today? Have you ever encountered Christ in or through a stranger? The worshipper is invited to contemplate 10 photographs of different kinds of people.

Station 6: Breaking bread [Luke 24: 30-31]
A loaf of bread on a table, flanked by candles and an open art book showing Caravaggio's painting of the moment when Christ breaks the bread and is recognised by the two disciples. The picture is also projected on the wall behind the station. There is a meditation about recognizing Christ; there are many copies of this to take away. Worshippers break and eat pieces of the bread.

Station 7: Burning hearts [Luke 24: 32-35]
How are you going to tell others about Christ? How will you express your faith to others? There is a short piece of writing to think upon, and worshippers are invited to light candles and pray for others.

This liturgy concluded the worship:

Jesus himself came and walked along with them but they were kept from recognising him.
So often present but hidden, hidden but present. Is it us not seeing or you not revealing?
Help us through dark nights and thin places to see you and to know you
Let our story be part of your story

They stood still their faces downcast
Lord you come out of the depths of depression, boredom, aloneness, lost hope.
Lift our hearts and minds
Untrouble our hearts.
Let our story be part of your story

And beginning with Moses and the prophets he explained to them what was said in all the scriptures concerning himself.
Help us share our stories, feelings, reactions, hopes, doubts and joys with each other and you.
Let our story be part of your story

Stay with us for it is nearly evening. The day is almost over.
Lord we encounter you sometimes through the everyday.

And sometimes through the unexpected, the
uncomfortable, the stranger.
We welcome Jesus the stranger
Let our journey be part of your journey

*When he was at the table with them he took bread, gave
thanks, broke it and began to give it to them. Then their
eyes were opened.*
Was it the way you broke bread?
The way you spoke?
Open our eyes
Open our hearts
Let our story be part of your story

Were not our hearts burning within us?
The beginning of an adventure
Let our adventure be part of your adventure

The Sin of Holiness

God we come to you as we are in unholiness and in holiness; as sinners and as children of God.

We are sorry for the times when we are not holy, when we have put barriers between ourselves and you.
Forgive us Lord

We are sorry for the times when we set a measure or standard of holiness to aspire to that is not what you require of us.
Forgive us Lord

Thank you Jesus that you shattered the illusion of the Pharisees' holiness. You re-interpreted holiness. Despite being accused of being a glutton and drunkard, you engaged with sinners, those on the edges, the poor, the needy, the sick, Roman officials, tax collectors, prostitutes, lepers, the rich, rulers, and widows. We could think of many types of people who you would be engaged with today*.

Let us not abstain from engaging with the world.
Let us not commit the sin of holiness.
Amen

* Modern alternatives:

upper class, elderly, singles, gamblers, ethnic minorities, gypsies, homosexuals, the homeless, unemployed, the dying, single parents, clergy, aids sufferers, business executives, paedophiles, families, politicians, the low paid, ex-convicts, alcoholics…

Men Of Doubt

[inspired by sitting in church one morning and feeling unable to join in the song *Men of Faith*]

Men of doubt you don't need to rise up and sing
We know that your doubt is actually an important part of
faith and it is important to be honest and real in your
journey of faith rather than pretend.
It's part of the mystery of God's way that when you are
weak there is strength
And God is close to you when you feel broken....

So you really don't need to shout to the north.
It's enough to sit down quietly and be here - (in fact it
would be enough to not even be here)
Be yourself, be real - you are loved.
Christ is with you.

And women who are not sure quite where you are at you
don't need to stand and sing either.
It is ok for you to just be here (or take a week off - you
deserve it!)
You do so much, you carry so many things - family,
friends, work and so on.
So you don't need to carry God's people as well.

God is the God who heals - leave it to God.

So don't worry about shouting (unless that's your thing).
Just be in God's presence.
Let God renew your strength.

We've all struggled.
We've all experienced God changing us.
Deep down we all love God and want to journey with God.

So Church you can also relax.
You are broken so just be real.
Whether you sing or shout or sit quietly isn't what God is
worried about.
Keep on in the journey of faith and God's grace will
sustain you.

Three Is The Magic Number

Three is the magic number
Calling us out of individualism
Insisting on relationship
I to you
We to another
Trinity seeding networks
Until all the cosmos joins in

One to create
One to save
One to sustain

One to author
One to fight
One to enliven

One to conceive
One to die
One to resurrect

One to plan
One to act
One to explain

One's sufficient

Two's company
Three's community

Trinity expose our self-reliance
Trinity break open our exclusivity
Trinity seed our joining tonight

Amen

Trinity Wristband

The instructions below are to make a wristband out of three cords with a bead interwoven into the band. We used this on Trinity Sunday to be a reminder of the Trinity and us being included in that relationship.

You need:

3 strands of embroidery silk each about 75cm; small safety pin; small bead

1. Knot the three strands together about 5 cm from one end. Use the safety pin to attach this knot to your trousers or skirt just above your knee.

2. Spread the strands out and mentally number them 1,2, and 3

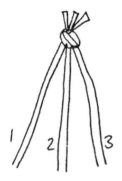

3. Hold strand 2 taut with your left hand. With your right hand knot strand 1 around strand 2. Pull strand 1 upwards tightly to knot it around strand 2.

4 Let go of strand 2. Hold strand 3 taut with your left hand.
With your right hand knot strand 1 around strand 3. Again
pull strand 1 upwards tightly to knot it around strand 3.
Knotting strand 1 around strands 2 and 3 means only the
colour of strand 1 is visible in the knot. The key to a good
wristband is to hold strands 2 and 3 taut.

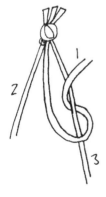

5. Leave strand 1 to the right of the other two. Mentally
renumber them from the left 1,2,3, and start again. If the

wristband twists, just untwist it remembering which order the colours are in.

6. After 3 cm of wristband put the bead on one of the strands and knot around it. This represents you being included in the relationship of the Trinity. Stop when the wristband is about 12cm long. Knot the end and tie round your wrist.

God Is Not Far From Us

God is not far from us

In God we live and move and have our being

Draw near to God and God will draw near to you

In God we live and move and have our being

God is the One who gives us the breath of life

In God we live and move and have our being

God has shared in our life

We are invited to share in God's life

In God we live and move and have our being

Snowhole

In the snowhole between endings and new beginnings
Christ comes to us bearing soup.
He has waited for us patiently
a day's journey from certainty in any direction,
where the peaks surrounding cities walled against him
rise into a sky whose meaning is not fixed.

Unique But Together

Lord we thank you that we are fearfully and
wonderfully made.
You formed us each in your own image, and you made us
all special
Our voices, our faces, our bodies, our habits, our talents,
and our failings
All the same and all unique

You search me and you know me,
You search us and you know us

We each have our private stories, feelings, our places, our
hopes, our joys,
Our secret fears, resentments, insecurities, doubts
which we bear alone or we bear together
Help us to hold our individuality
with our place in community

Search me and know me,
Search us and know us

Jesus you walked alone in the desert,
You shared a life and ministry with your twelve disciples
You were surrounded by massive crowds,

You spoke to individuals and to multitudes
You suffered alone on the cross,

Search me and know me
Search us and know us

We come to you as individuals,
We come to you as a community
In the silence of night, the brightness of morning,
the turbulence of the rush hour,
In this church building, in our workplaces, and homes

Help us to be one with ourselves,
one with each other and one with you   Amen

Mountain:Valley:Plain

To stand on the peaks of mountains is not a given. Helicopter flights are expensive, and the highest peaks are out of their reach. To climb a mountain will require total commitment to the journey, careful preparation, and technical skills. For much of the climb there will be no great views, only struggle and necessary concentration on the task at hand. It is, of course, possible at any time to say "enough", take what enjoyment you can, and start back down; but to do so is to miss the best.

On top of the mountain the trees and clouds are below us, and the sun blazes in an azure sky. For a while after we descend, the resulting tan will mark us out as having been in the mountains, like the fading radiance of Moses' face. Meanwhile we stop for a while, dazzled by light and space, seeing familiar landmarks from an unfamiliar angle, excited by new vistas that open before us like welcoming arms.

The top of the mountain is a place for seeing clearly the lie of the land through which we must journey, for understanding the relationship of the places we have been and the places we are going to next, and perhaps for glimpsing our final destination, if the air is clear enough.

We drink in the view, trying to fix it in our minds, knowing that we will not see so far in the thicker air below.

Our time on the summit is necessarily limited. It is not possible to live on top of a mountain, except by destroying the qualities that made it desirable in the first place. But the memory of the view will remain long after the horizons have closed in on descent, and we will recognise the other mountains and the far-off places when we come to them, having seen them once before and carried them within us through the valleys and plains.

The far side of the mountain is often a place of cold shadow, and we will think wistfully of the sun and space we left behind. Avalanches and cliffs imperil us, sudden and violent storms blind and overwhelm us. The ground crumbles beneath our feet, and snowfields hide crevasses under a thin smiling crust. The mountains, which shone around us like laughter as we climbed, now shut out the sun, and the valley is bleak and shelterless. We are exhausted, frozen, soaked to the skin, and each hard step brings the choice of whether to live or die - for to stop is to die, and yet to keep moving is to suffer. Even if we live, parts of us may freeze and die here, and we will bear the scars for the rest of our journey.

But every valley contains a river or contains the memory of a river, if you have eyes to see. And the river that shattered the rocks and flayed the mountainside will nourish the plains when its violence is spent. The debris of the broken mountain will form the fertile mud of the plains, cast down in the riverbends that swing through the fields like lazy childbearing hips.

When the tan has faded, when the scars have healed, when the stories have been told in the pub and at dinner parties, what we call normal life will resume. It is characteristic of normal life that it denies the possibility of things being different - this is how life is, it says, how it always was and always will be. Why wish for anything else? Why waste your time on dreams? But the mountains and the valleys will not be denied, and those who have known them carry a secret within them. Like a Tardis, they stand in the corner looking normal. But they are bigger inside than out.

Stones and Water: A Meditation

Seat people in circles of 5-10 people. Give each person a stone or pebble.

Ask everyone to sit in silence with their eyes closed and invite them to feel their particular stone to 'get to know' it.

Read these words:
Jesus said "Let anyone who is thirsty come to me. Let anyone who is thirsty come to me and drink. As the scripture says 'From their heart shall flow streams of living water'"

"When they came to Jesus, they saw he was already dead, and so instead of breaking his legs one of the soldiers came and pierced his side with a lance and immediately there came out blood and water."

Meister Eckhart said "God is a great underground river that no one can dam up and no one can stop"

Allow time to consider these words and take them on a journey...

Imagine your stone lying in the bed of a dried up stream. Suddenly the water starts to flow again like the water from the side of the crucified Christ. A river of love washes over you. The dirt around you in the stream bed is washed away. The water, the love flows around you, ever faster. The river of love sweeps you along knocking you against other stones, against rocks, swirling sand around you. Slowly, slowly over many years the river wears away your rough spots and imperfections shaping you to its will. Yet the stones are not all the same. Jesus said "every hair on your head has been counted". All stones may seem alike but by now you should know your stone well without looking at it. Keeping your eyes shut pass your stone to the person on your right. Now keep passing the stones until you feel that your original stone has come back to you. Jesus said " I know my own and my own know me, just as the Father knows me and I know the Father".

Index